BODY
DYSMORPHIC
DISORDER WORKBOOK

A Transformative Journey to Cultivating Positive Body Image and Unshakeable Confidence"

EDWIN C. KING

Copyright page

1

Dedication

To those who wake up each day and face the mirror with courage, despite the inner battles with Body Dysmorphic Disorder, this book is dedicated to you. Your journey is one of incredible bravery and resilience, and it is my hope that these pages provide comfort, understanding, and practical guidance on your path to self-acceptance.

To the loved ones who offer a steady hand, a listening ear, and a compassionate heart, thank you for being the unwavering support system for those navigating the complexities of BDD. Your patience and love make a profound difference in their lives.

To the mental health professionals who tirelessly work to shed light on the shadows of BDD, your dedication and empathy pave the way for healing and understanding. Your efforts are deeply appreciated by all who have been touched by this disorder.

And to the reader, whether you are seeking help, offering support, or simply trying to understand, thank you for taking this step. May you find within these pages the strength, hope, and insight to overcome the challenges ahead. Together, we can break the silence and stigma surrounding Body Dysmorphic Disorder.

Acknowledgments

Writing this book has been a journey of discovery, reflection, and immense growth. It would not have been possible without the support, guidance, and inspiration of many individuals who have contributed to its creation.

First and foremost, I would like to express my deepest gratitude to the individuals who shared their personal experiences with Body Dysmorphic Disorder. Your bravery and openness have provided invaluable insights and have shaped this book in profound ways. Thank you for trusting me with your stories.

A heartfelt thank you to my family and friends for your endless support and encouragement. Your belief in me, even during the most challenging times, has been a source of strength and motivation. I am especially grateful to my [specific family members, friends, or mentors], whose unwavering faith in my work has been a guiding light.

To my editor, prof. Kenneth Edward, thank you for your keen insights, meticulous attention to detail, and unwavering dedication to bringing this book to life. Your expertise and guidance have been invaluable throughout this process.

Finally, to my readers, thank you for embarking on this journey with me. Whether you are someone affected by BDD, a loved one, a mental health professional, or simply someone seeking to understand, your willingness to learn and grow alongside this book is deeply appreciated.

Table

Of contents

introduction

Imagine walking through life with a mirror that distorts your image into something unrecognizable, magnifying every perceived flaw until it overshadows your entire perception of self. This is the daily reality for those battling Body Dysmorphic Disorder (BDD)—a reality that was all too familiar for James, a young architect I worked with. Despite his striking features and professional success, James saw only deformities and imperfections when he looked in the mirror. His fixation on these imagined flaws led him to avoid important career opportunities and social events, isolating him in a world governed by his own critical eye.

As a therapist that is well experienced in body image issues, I've encountered numerous cases of Body Dysmorphic Disorder (BDD), each with its unique challenges and complexities. Another memorable case was that of Anna, a young graphic designer who came to my office draped in oversized clothes, her demeanor fraught with anxiety. She confessed that she had spent the last three hours applying makeup to cover what she described as "horrendous skin." In reality, her skin appeared normal, with barely noticeable blemishes. Anna's case was severe; she avoided mirrors and windows and had started working from home to escape the gaze of colleagues, whom she believed were constantly judging her appearance.

Anna's story is not uncommon among individuals with BDD. This disorder is characterized by an obsessive focus on one or more perceived flaws in appearance, flaws that are either minor or invisible to others. People with BDD can spend hours fixating on their reflection, engaging in repetitive behaviors like skin picking, or seeking numerous cosmetic procedures, which provide only temporary relief, if any.

What is Body Dysmorphic Disorder?

Body Dysmorphic Disorder (BDD) is a mental health condition that causes a person to be excessively concerned about perceived defects in their physical appearance, which are often unnoticeable to others. Classified under the Obsessive-Compulsive and Related Disorders in the DSM-5, BDD involves a distressing and sometimes debilitating preoccupation with appearance. This can manifest in hours spent fixating in front of a mirror, or in extreme cases, avoiding mirrors altogether. It often leads to repeated cosmetic procedures, severe anxiety, and a profound feeling of inadequacy.

The Essential Role of This Workbook

This workbook is designed as a crucial resource for those like James, who are fighting to reclaim their lives from BDD. It offers practical tools and insights that have been proven effective in clinical practice. Through expert advice, and evidence-based exercises, readers will gain a comprehensive understanding of BDD. More importantly, they will learn actionable strategies to manage and overcome the disorder. Each chapter builds on the last, providing a structured path towards greater self-acceptance and mental resilience.

Why This Book Matters

The journey to overcoming BDD is fraught with challenges and setbacks. However, with the right guidance and support, it is entirely possible to lead a fulfilling life, free from the shackles of obsessive self-scrutiny. This book aims to equip readers with the knowledge and tools necessary for this journey, offering hope and empowerment to those who have often felt misunderstood or helpless.

As we delve deeper into understanding BDD and its impacts, this workbook will serve as your guide, illuminating the path to recovery with both compassion and expertise. Whether you are battling BDD yourself, supporting a loved one, or are a professional seeking effective interventions, this workbook is an invaluable asset in navigating the complexities of this disorder.

Through real-life stories like that of James, expertly blended with therapeutic insights, this workbook not only educates but also inspires. It provides not just hope, but a concrete plan for those looking to overcome the debilitating effects of Body Dysmorphic Disorder. This is your first step towards a life defined not by your appearance, but by your resilience and strength.

Historical Context and Evolution of BDD

Body Dysmorphic Disorder (BDD) may appear to be a relatively modern phenomenon, particularly given today's intense focus on appearance and media imagery. However, the disorder has a much longer history, with its understanding and recognition evolving significantly over time.

Early Observations

The earliest accounts resembling BDD symptoms date back to the 19th century. The disorder was first clinically described by the Italian psychiatrist Enrico Morselli in 1891 under the term "dysmorphophobia," which he defined as "an objective ugliness felt as an overestimation of the proportions or fantasies of ugliness." Morselli's observations marked the beginning of recognizing BDD as a distinct psychiatric condition, characterized by an excessive preoccupation with a perceived defect in physical appearance.

20th Century Developments

During the early to mid-20th century, understanding of BDD remained relatively stagnant, with few clinicians distinguishing the symptoms from those of other psychiatric disorders such as obsessive-compulsive disorder (OCD) or depression. It was not until the latter part of the century that BDD began to emerge as a separate diagnostic category. Researchers and clinicians started to document cases where individuals, despite normal appearance, were preoccupied with imagined defects or minor flaws.

In 1987, the American Psychiatric Association officially recognized BDD in the third edition of the Diagnostic and Statistical Manual of Mental Disorders (DSM-III-R), under the category of "atypical somatoform disorder." This inclusion marked a significant milestone in the history of BDD, acknowledging it as a legitimate and serious mental health issue.

Modern Understanding

The understanding of BDD has expanded significantly with the advent of the DSM-IV and DSM-5. These more recent editions have provided clearer diagnostic criteria and have distinguished BDD more clearly from other disorders like OCD and eating disorders. The DSM-5 categorizes BDD in the obsessive-compulsive spectrum, highlighting its obsessive and compulsive traits.

Research into BDD has also grown, exploring its causes, which include genetic, neurobiological, and environmental factors. Studies have shown that BDD often co-occurs with other mental health disorders, such as major depression and anxiety disorders, which has implications for treatment strategies.

Treatment Evolution

Treatment methodologies have evolved from purely psychoanalytic approaches to more diversified and evidence-based treatments. Cognitive Behavioral Therapy (CBT), which focuses on altering distorted beliefs and behaviors related to one's body image, has become the gold standard in BDD treatment. Medications, particularly selective serotonin reuptake inhibitors (SSRIs), have also been found effective, especially in severe cases.

Additionally, the rise of digital technology and social media has both complicated and advanced the understanding of BDD. These platforms can exacerbate concerns over appearance but also provide new venues for therapy and support, including online therapy sessions and support groups.

Looking Forward

The journey from the initial recognition of BDD as dysmorphophobia to a well-recognized clinical diagnosis illustrates the evolving understanding of mental health. Continuous research and clinical practice are expanding what we know about BDD, improving treatment outcomes, and providing hope to those affected. As awareness grows, so too does the ability to identify and effectively treat this debilitating disorder, helping individuals to lead fuller, less fear-driven lives.

This historical context not only highlights the progression in the understanding and treatment of BDD but also underscores the importance of continued research and adaptation in approaches to mental health. The journey of understanding BDD is far from complete, and this workbook is part of that ongoing evolution, offering current insights and practical strategies based on the latest research.

The Spectrum of BDD: Mild to Severe Cases

Body Dysmorphic Disorder (BDD) manifests along a spectrum, from mild preoccupations with appearance to severe and debilitating obsessions that can dominate a person's life. Understanding this spectrum is crucial for both diagnosis and treatment. Throughout my experience as a therapist, I have encountered numerous cases that illustrate the wide range of severity in BDD symptoms. Here are some examples to illuminate this spectrum:

Mild Cases of BDD

Case Example: Tom

Tom, a college student, came to therapy concerned about his hair. He believed that it looked excessively thin and spent about 30 minutes daily styling it to cover perceived bald spots. Tom was still able to attend classes and socialize, but his worries about his hair were a persistent source of stress, leading him to avoid certain outdoor activities where he couldn't control his appearance, like swimming or windy conditions.

In mild BDD, individuals like Tom are often able to function relatively well in their daily lives but experience significant distress over specific perceived flaws. The preoccupation does not consume their entire day, and they may respond well to a combination of brief cognitive behavioral therapy and minimal medication, or even lifestyle adjustments.

Moderate Cases of BDD

Case Example: Lisa

Lisa, a graphic designer in her early 30s, was excessively concerned about her complexion, which she perceived as severely scarred and uneven, although in reality, her skin had only mild acne marks. Lisa spent over an hour every day applying makeup and frequently cancelled meetings or dates if she felt she couldn't conceal her perceived flaws sufficiently. Her work performance began to suffer as she avoided video calls and in-person presentations.

Moderate BDD involves more significant interference with the person's daily life and mental health. The obsessions might result in frequent avoidance of social situations and considerable distress, often requiring more intensive treatment such as regular therapy sessions, possibly combined with a longer-term medication strategy.

Severe Cases of BDD

Case Example: Emily

Emily, a 28-year-old teacher, had severe BDD focusing on her nose, which she perceived as grotesquely misshapen. This obsession led her to undergo multiple cosmetic surgeries, none of which alleviated her distress. Emily spent several hours a day examining her face in various mirrors, had withdrawn from all social activities, and eventually took a leave of absence from her job. Her life was controlled by rituals of checking and rechecking her appearance and seeking reassurance from others, which never satisfied her need for certainty about her looks.

In severe BDD, like Emily's case, individuals may become almost entirely incapacitated by their disorder. They often require intensive treatment, which might include inpatient care, more aggressive pharmacological treatment, and long-term, intensive psychotherapy focusing on managing the disorder and improving functional living.

The spectrum of BDD illustrates that while the core symptoms may be consistent—obsessive thoughts about perceived appearance flaws—the impact on one's life can vary dramatically. Effective treatment is often tailored to where individuals fall on this spectrum, emphasizing the need for personalized therapy and support.

Through these examples, it's evident that BDD can take many forms, affecting people differently. Recognizing the severity and the specific needs of each case allows for more effective interventions and supports the broader goal of this workbook: to provide a framework that helps readers navigate their journey through BDD, from mild worries to severe disruptions.

Chapter 1

Self-Assessment and Early Detection

Early detection of Body Dysmorphic Disorder (BDD) is crucial for effective intervention and management. Self-assessment tools can play a vital role in recognizing potential signs of BDD. These questionnaires are not diagnostic tools but can help individuals identify symptoms that may warrant professional evaluation. Below are detailed questionnaires designed to help readers assess their concerns about appearance and determine if these concerns might align with symptoms of BDD.

BDD Self-Assessment Questionnaire

This questionnaire is designed to help you assess whether you might have symptoms consistent with Body Dysmorphic Disorder. Answer the following questions honestly. Remember, this is not a substitute for a professional diagnosis but can help guide you towards seeking appropriate help if needed.

1. Preoccupation with Appearance:

- Do you find that you spend a lot of time worrying about one or more aspects of your appearance?
- Are there specific features you dislike or feel are not right, despite others telling you they look normal?

2. Repetitive Behaviors:

- Do you engage in behaviors aimed at checking, fixing, or hiding what you perceive as flaws? (e.g., frequently checking mirrors, skin picking, excessive grooming)
- How much time do you spend on these behaviors daily?

3. Impact on Daily Life:

- Have your concerns about your appearance caused you significant distress or problems in your social life, work, or other areas?

- Do you avoid social situations, work, or public places because you feel self-conscious about your appearance?

4. Emotional Distress:
- Do these concerns make you feel depressed, anxious, or very ashamed of yourself?
- Have you ever felt so bad about your appearance that you've thought about harming yourself or felt you'd be better off dead?

5. Perceived Defects:
- When you discuss your appearance concerns with others, do they seem minor or nonexistent to them?
- Do you believe that people take special notice of your appearance in a negative way or mock you?

6. Cosmetic Procedures:
- Have you sought cosmetic procedures to alter your perceived flaws? If so, were you satisfied with the results?

- Do you feel compelled to undergo repeated procedures?

Scoring the Questionnaire

0-2 "Yes" answers: It is unlikely that you have BDD, but if you have concerns about your mental health, consulting a professional can be beneficial.

3-4 "Yes" answers: You may have mild to moderate symptoms of BDD. Consulting with a mental health professional for a detailed evaluation could be helpful.

5-6 "Yes" answers: Your answers suggest that you might have moderate to severe symptoms of BDD. It is advisable to seek a comprehensive evaluation from a mental health professional.

Importance of Professional Evaluation

While this questionnaire can help identify potential symptoms of BDD, it is essential to undergo a professional evaluation for an accurate diagnosis.

Mental health professionals use detailed clinical interviews and diagnostic criteria from the DSM-5 to determine whether an individual has BDD. They can also provide or recommend appropriate treatment, including therapy and medication.

Recognizing the signs of Body Dysmorphic Disorder through self-assessment is a critical first step towards seeking help. If you suspect that you or someone you know might be suffering from BDD, use this questionnaire as a preliminary tool, but always follow up with a professional assessment to ensure accurate diagnosis and effective treatment. This proactive approach is crucial in managing BDD and improving quality of life.

The Importance of Early Intervention

In the preceding sections, we discussed recognizing the early signs and symptoms of Body Dysmorphic Disorder (BDD) and introduced tools for self-assessment. Building on this foundation, it's crucial to understand why early intervention is not just beneficial but essential in managing and treating BDD effectively.

Enhancing Treatment Efficacy

Early intervention in BDD significantly enhances the efficacy of treatment. When BDD symptoms are addressed promptly, before deeply ingrained patterns of behavior and thought become established, interventions such as Cognitive Behavioral Therapy (CBT) can be more effective. Early treatment can prevent the disorder from escalating to a point where it leads to severe depression, anxiety, or even suicidal ideation, which are common in untreated or late-treated cases.

Preventing Progression and Complications

As explored through the personal journeys shared earlier, like James and Lisa's stories, we see how untreated BDD can lead to a cascade of complications, affecting social, professional, and personal spheres. Early intervention can halt this progression, preventing the disorder from causing profound social withdrawal, relationship breakdowns, and occupational impairment. For instance, if Lisa had sought help when she first began spending an excessive amount of time on makeup, she might have avoided the escalation of her symptoms, which ultimately impacted her professional life and self-esteem.

Reducing the Risk of Co-morbidity

BDD often coexists with other psychiatric disorders, such as depression and anxiety. Early detection and treatment of BDD can reduce the risk and severity of these co-morbid conditions. Addressing BDD symptoms early can interrupt the cycle of negative self-perception and obsessive behaviors before these patterns reinforce or trigger additional psychiatric conditions.

Cost-Effectiveness of Early Intervention

From a practical standpoint, early intervention is cost-effective. It can reduce the need for more intensive and prolonged treatment options that are required for severe cases. For example, multiple costly and potentially risky cosmetic surgeries often sought by individuals with severe BDD can be avoided if the disorder is managed effectively at an early stage.

Improving Long-Term Outcomes

The long-term outcomes for individuals with BDD improve dramatically with early intervention. When individuals receive treatment before the disorder deeply embeds itself into their daily routines and thought processes, they have a better prognosis. They are more likely to maintain stable relationships, perform effectively at work or school, and engage in social activities, contributing to a higher overall quality of life.

The journey through understanding and managing BDD underscores the transformative power of early intervention. As we continue to explore the facets of BDD in this workbook, remember that the goal is not just to treat BDD but to do so in a way that restores and enhances the individual's life. Early intervention is the cornerstone of this process, providing a beacon of hope and a practical path forward for those affected by this challenging disorder. By addressing BDD early, we not only alleviate the immediate symptoms but also pave the way for a healthier, more fulfilling future.

Chapter 2

Understanding the Psychology Behind BDD

Body Dysmorphic Disorder (BDD) is deeply rooted in cognitive distortions—ways in which an individual's thinking can become biased or inaccurate, particularly regarding self-image and body perception. These distortions significantly influence the severity and persistence of BDD, and understanding them is crucial for effective treatment and management. This section explores the key cognitive distortions associated with BDD, helping to illuminate why individuals with this disorder perceive themselves so differently from how others see them.

Common Cognitive Distortions in BDD

1. All-or-Nothing Thinking
Individuals with BDD often engage in all-or-nothing thinking, also known as dichotomous thinking. For example, they might believe that if

they do not have a perfect complexion, they are utterly unattractive. This type of thinking leaves no room for middle ground or varying degrees of beauty, which can exacerbate dissatisfaction with one's appearance.

2. Overgeneralization

This occurs when a person with BDD takes a small, perhaps negligible flaw and generalizes it to their entire appearance. For instance, a minor blemish might lead someone to conclude that they are completely flawed or hideous.

3. Catastrophizing

Catastrophizing involves anticipating the worst possible outcome from a perceived flaw. For example, someone with BDD might believe that a barely noticeable scar will lead to social isolation and lifelong unhappiness. This severe anxiety and fear can drive many of the compulsive behaviors seen in BDD, such as excessive grooming or mirror checking.

4. Emotional Reasoning

People with BDD often believe that their emotional reaction to their appearance reflects reality. If they feel ugly, they conclude that they must indeed be ugly, despite objective evidence to the contrary. This distortion makes it challenging to convince them of their actual appearance through reassurance from others.

5. Mind Reading

This distortion involves assuming what others are thinking without any factual basis. An individual with BDD might believe that others are focusing on and negatively judging their perceived flaws, even though there is no evidence to support this belief.

6. Self-Imposed Standards

Extremely high and often unrealistic standards of beauty are set by individuals with BDD. Any deviation from these standards is unacceptable, reinforcing their negative self-view and driving further dissatisfaction and preoccupation with appearance.

The Impact of Cognitive Distortions

These cognitive distortions can severely impact one's quality of life, leading to behaviors that reinforce the BDD cycle. For example, frequent mirror checking might temporarily relieve anxiety but ultimately reinforces the distorted beliefs and rituals. Understanding these distortions is not only key for those affected by BDD but also for therapists and support networks in providing effective support and interventions.

Understanding the psychological underpinnings of BDD through the lens of cognitive distortions provides vital insights into the disorder's nature and its treatment. This knowledge not only helps individuals affected by BDD but also equips therapists and caregivers with the tools necessary for effective intervention, setting the stage for recovery and improved well-being. As we explore further into BDD in this workbook, these foundational insights will guide our approach to managing and ultimately overcoming the disorder.

Psychological Theories Explaining BDD

Understanding Body Dysmorphic Disorder (BDD) requires an exploration into the psychological theories that explain its origins and persistence. These theories provide a framework for understanding how BDD develops and is maintained, offering crucial insights that inform effective treatment strategies. Here, we delve into several key psychological theories that help explain the mechanisms behind BDD.

1. Cognitive Behavioral Theory

The cognitive-behavioral perspective is central to understanding BDD. This theory suggests that BDD arises from maladaptive thought patterns and beliefs about one's appearance, coupled with problematic behavioral responses. Individuals with BDD typically have distorted beliefs about their looks, which lead to excessive self-scrutiny and avoidance behaviors. Cognitive distortions, such as all-or-nothing thinking, overgeneralization, and catastrophizing, play a significant role in sustaining these beliefs.

Cognitive aspects: Focus on perceived defects and magnification of their importance.

Behavioral aspects: Engaging in compulsive behaviors like checking mirrors or excessive grooming.

Cognitive-behavioral therapy (CBT), which helps individuals challenge and change these distortions and behaviors, is considered one of the most effective treatments for BDD

2. Biopsychosocial Model

This model provides a comprehensive approach by considering biological, psychological, and social factors in the development and maintenance of BDD.

Biological factors: Genetic predispositions and neurobiological abnormalities may contribute to the onset of BDD. Research suggests that certain areas of the brain related to processing visual information and emotional regulation may function differently in individuals with BDD.

Psychological factors: Personality traits such as perfectionism and neuroticism, and a history of trauma or abuse can increase susceptibility to developing BDD.

Social factors: Cultural and societal pressures emphasizing physical appearance, along with specific life events, such as bullying or teasing about appearance, are significant in the development of BDD.

This holistic view encourages treatments that address multiple aspects of the individual's life, including medical interventions, psychological therapy, and social support systems.

3. Psychoanalytic Theory

Although less emphasized in contemporary treatment, the psychoanalytic theory offers another perspective on BDD. It suggests that BDD symptoms may be a manifestation of deeper, unresolved conflicts or traumas. According to this view, obsessions with physical appearance may symbolically represent deeper psychological issues or serve as a displacement for internal conflicts.

Treatment from this perspective may involve exploring unconscious conflicts, childhood experiences, and significant relationships that could be contributing to the symptoms of BDD.

4. Evolutionary Psychology

Some theorists have applied evolutionary psychology to explain why BDD might occur. They suggest that an intense focus on appearance could be an exaggerated form of an adaptive focus on social status and mating prospects, which are influenced by physical attractiveness. This theory posits that BDD may represent an evolutionary mismatch, where natural vigilance for social acceptance through appearance becomes pathological.

These theories, each highlighting different facets of BDD, are not mutually exclusive and often overlap in their explanations and treatment implications. Understanding these varied perspectives allows for a richer, more nuanced approach to treatment. It underscores the complexity of BDD and the need for personalized treatment plans that consider the unique psychological makeup and life history of each individual.

In the context of this workbook, these theories not only enrich our understanding but also guide the structuring of interventions, aiming to address the underlying psychological roots of BDD and providing a pathway towards recovery.

The Role of Self-Image and Identity in BDD

Self-image and identity play central roles in Body Dysmorphic Disorder (BDD), profoundly influencing how individuals perceive themselves and interact with the world. BDD can be seen as a disorder where the distortion of self-image and the obsessive concern with appearance are at the forefront, affecting the person's overall identity and sense of self-worth. Understanding the interplay between self-image and identity can provide deeper insights into the mechanisms of BDD and enhance therapeutic approaches.

Distorted Self-Image

In BDD, the self-image—how one perceives and feels about one's appearance—is significantly distorted. Individuals with BDD often have a highly critical, negative view of their physical self, focusing excessively on perceived flaws or defects that are either minor or nonexistent to others. This distorted self-image is persistent and resistant to contrary evidence or reassurance from others.

Magnification of Flaws: People with BDD tend to magnify small imperfections, often interpreting them as a significant part of their physical identity.

Misinterpretation of Others' Views: Individuals with BDD commonly believe that others view them as unattractive or deformed, which reinforces their distorted self-image.

Identity and BDD

Identity in BDD is often overly tied to physical appearance. For individuals suffering from BDD, their sense of self often revolves around how they look, overshadowing other qualities and achievements.

Self-Worth Dependent on Appearance: Self-esteem is overly dependent on appearance, rather than a more balanced view that includes personal, social, and intellectual attributes.

*Role Conflicts: Individuals with BDD may struggle with their roles in relationships, work, and society because their preoccupation with appearance distracts from their abilities to perform or engage in various social roles.

Psychological Impact

The impact of a distorted self-image and identity on a person's psychological health can be profound:

Social Withdrawal: Due to embarrassment or fear of judgment about their appearance, individuals with BDD often avoid social interactions, leading to isolation and loneliness.

Anxiety and Depression: The constant preoccupation with appearance and perceived inadequacy can lead to high levels of anxiety and severe depression, sometimes culminating in suicidal thoughts or actions.

In BDD, the distorted self-image and the consequent impact on identity are central to both the experience and the treatment of the disorder. Effective therapy addresses these aspects by helping individuals recognize and adjust their self-perceptions and by broadening their identity beyond physical appearance. This approach not only alleviates the symptoms of BDD but also enhances overall well-being and functionality, guiding individuals toward a more balanced and fulfilling life. As we explore further in this workbook, these insights into self-image and identity will underpin our strategies for overcoming the challenges posed by BDD.

Chapter 3

Biological and Environmental Influences on BDD

In our comprehensive exploration of Body Dysmorphic Disorder (BDD), it is crucial to understand the multifaceted origins of the disorder, which include both biological and environmental components. This section delves into the genetic predispositions and biological factors that contribute to BDD, illustrating how these elements interplay with psychological and environmental factors to influence the development and progression of the disorder.

Genetic Predispositions

Research indicates that BDD may have a genetic component, suggesting that susceptibility to the disorder can be inherited. Studies involving twins and families show a higher concordance rate for BDD among monozygotic (identical) twins compared to dizygotic (fraternal) twins, underscoring the potential role of genetic factors.

Family History: Individuals with a family history of BDD or related disorders, such as obsessive-compulsive disorder (OCD) or depression, are at a heightened risk of developing BDD. This suggests some shared genetic pathways between these disorders.

Heritability Studies: Genetic studies have begun to identify specific genes that might be associated with an increased risk of BDD, although this research is still in its early stages. These genes often relate to the regulation of serotonin and dopamine, neurotransmitters involved in mood regulation and reward processing.

Biological Factors

Beyond genetics, various biological factors have been implicated in the onset and maintenance of BDD. These include neurobiological differences and hormonal influences that may affect perception, mood, and behavior.

Brain Structure and Function: Neuroimaging studies have shown that individuals with BDD may have abnormalities in certain areas of the brain, particularly those involved in visual processing and executive control. For example, alterations in the orbitofrontal cortex, which is involved in decision-making and behavioral responses, and the amygdala, a center for emotional reactions, may contribute to the obsessive and compulsive traits seen in BDD.

Neurotransmitter Systems: Dysregulation in neurotransmitter systems, especially serotonin, is commonly observed in BDD, similar to other obsessive-compulsive spectrum disorders. This dysregulation can affect mood, anxiety levels, and obsessive thoughts.

Hormonal Influences: While less studied, hormonal changes or imbalances might also play a role in BDD, particularly during periods of significant hormonal fluctuation such as adolescence or menopause, which can coincide with the onset or exacerbation of BDD symptoms.

The intersection of genetic and biological factors with environmental and psychological influences forms a complex framework that explains the development of BDD. By recognizing these foundational elements, we can better understand the varied manifestations of BDD and tailor interventions more effectively. This holistic view not only informs clinical approaches but also underscores the importance of addressing a broad spectrum of influences in treatment plans. As we continue to unravel the biological aspects of BDD, integrating these findings with therapeutic practices remains essential in providing effective care and improving outcomes for those affected by the disorder.

Societal and Cultural Influences on BDD

Body Dysmorphic Disorder (BDD) is profoundly influenced by societal and cultural factors, which shape individuals' perceptions of beauty and, consequently, their self-image. In this section, we explore how these external pressures contribute to the development and exacerbation of BDD, reflecting on the pervasive role of cultural norms and media portrayals in defining what is considered "ideal" or desirable in physical appearance.

Media Influence

The media plays a pivotal role in setting and perpetuating beauty standards. Through advertising, television, films, and, increasingly, social media, certain body types and features are highlighted and idealized, creating unrealistic benchmarks for beauty.

Idealized Images: Media often showcase highly curated and photoshopped images that set unrealistic standards for physical appearance. These images can lead to a distorted perception of what is normal or achievable, compelling individuals to strive for unattainable perfection.

Social Media Pressure: Platforms like Instagram and Facebook amplify exposure to idealized images. The interactive nature of these platforms, where users receive immediate feedback in the form of likes and comments, intensifies concerns over appearance and increases the risk of developing BDD.

Cultural Standards of Beauty

Cultural contexts deeply influence what is considered attractive, and these standards can vary significantly from one society to another. However, the globalization of media has led to a more homogenized view of beauty, often skewed toward Western ideals.

Cultural Diversity and Beauty Standards: While beauty standards differ globally, Western ideals often dominate due to the widespread consumption of Western media. This can create significant distress for individuals in non-Western cultures who feel they must conform to these external standards.

Cultural Practices and Rituals: In some cultures, certain body modifications and practices are considered essential for beauty, such as skin lightening, hair straightening, or body shaping.

These practices can reinforce the idea that natural physical features are inadequate or undesirable.

Societal Expectations and Criticism

Society often places a high value on physical appearance, linking it to success, happiness, and social acceptance. This creates an environment where individuals feel pressured to meet these expectations to avoid criticism or rejection.

Stigma and Judgment: People who do not conform to societal beauty standards may face judgment or discrimination, which can exacerbate feelings of inadequacy and propel the development of BDD.

Professional and Social Opportunities: Appearance can unfairly influence opportunities for employment and advancement, as well as social interactions, reinforcing the importance of beauty in societal success and acceptance.

The Role of Family and Peers

Family and peers also contribute to the development of body image concerns through their attitudes and behaviors regarding appearance.

Family Influence: Family members may unconsciously transmit societal beauty standards by emphasizing physical appearance or expressing dissatisfaction with their own or others' appearances.

Peer Comparisons Especially among adolescents and young adults, peer comparisons and comments about physical appearance can profoundly impact self-esteem and body image, potentially triggering or exacerbating BDD symptoms.

Societal and cultural influences are integral to understanding the etiology and persistence of BDD. They shape individuals' perceptions of themselves and their bodies, often fostering a chronic dissatisfaction and preoccupation with perceived flaws. Recognizing these influences allows for a more comprehensive approach to treating BDD, which should include addressing the societal and cultural pressures that patients experience. Interventions might involve promoting media literacy, enhancing self-esteem, and fostering a more inclusive and diverse representation of beauty standards, thereby helping individuals navigate and resist the pressures that contribute to BDD. This broader understanding not only enriches our approach within this workbook but also equips readers with the tools to critically assess and challenge the external factors that impact their self-image and well-being.

The Impact of Media and Technology on Body Dysmorphic Disorder (BDD)

In the digital age, the influence of media and technology on mental health and self-perception has become increasingly significant. For individuals vulnerable to or suffering from Body Dysmorphic Disorder (BDD), the pervasive presence of digital media can play a critical role in both triggering and exacerbating the condition. This section examines how modern media and technological advancements impact BDD, focusing on the ways they reshape individuals' engagements with body image and societal expectations.

The Role of Digital Media in Shaping Perceptions

Media, particularly digital media, serves as a powerful conduit for conveying and reinforcing beauty standards. The ubiquity and accessibility of this media mean that individuals are constantly bombarded with images and messages that promote often unattainable beauty ideals.

Social Media Platforms: Platforms like Instagram, TikTok, and Snapchat are known for their focus on visual content, which often includes filtered and edited images that present highly idealized versions of beauty. Regular exposure to such content can distort an individual's perception of normal body types and facial features, leading to increased dissatisfaction and preoccupation with one's appearance.

Advertising and Marketing: Digital marketing employs sophisticated targeting strategies that present cosmetic and fashion products alongside idealized images, creating associations between these products and the attainment of beauty ideals. This not only influences purchasing behaviors but also affects self-esteem and body image.

Technology's Double-Edged Sword

While technology has facilitated the spread of harmful beauty standards, it also offers tools that can both negatively and positively impact BDD symptoms.

Photo-editing and Filters: The widespread use of photo-editing apps and built-in camera filters allows users to alter their images to meet beauty standards before sharing them online. While this can temporarily boost self-esteem, it also reinforces unrealistic expectations and dissatisfaction with one's natural appearance.

Virtual and Augmented Reality: Emerging technologies like virtual reality (VR) and augmented reality (AR) offer new realms for experiencing and manipulating body image. These technologies can potentially intensify body image issues if used to perpetuate idealized body standards, but they also hold therapeutic potential if designed to promote body positivity and realistic beauty standards.

Cyberbullying and Online Culture

The anonymous or semi-anonymous nature of online interactions can lead to increased instances of cyberbullying, with harmful comments and feedback that can be particularly devastating for individuals with BDD.

Online Harassment   Negative or mocking comments about one's appearance on social media can significantly worsen BDD symptoms, leading to increased isolation, anxiety, and depression.

Social Comparison: Social media inherently encourages comparison, often leading to upward social comparison, where individuals compare themselves unfavorably to those they perceive as better or more attractive. This can exacerbate feelings of inadequacy and obsessions with appearance.

The relationship between media, technology, and BDD is complex and multifaceted. As we navigate this digital landscape, it is vital to understand both the risks and opportunities these tools present. By critically engaging with media and employing technology thoughtfully, we can mitigate its negative impacts and harness its potential for positive support. This understanding is crucial not only for individuals dealing with BDD but also for caregivers, therapists, and policymakers who are in a position to shape the digital environment in ways that promote mental health and well-being.

Chapter 4

Practical Approaches and Interactive Sections for BDD

In managing BDD, incorporating practical approaches that engage individuals actively in their recovery is crucial. This section of the workbook is dedicated to providing interactive exercises, practical advice, and professional insights that can be applied in daily life to manage and alleviate the symptoms of BDD.

Interactive Exercise: CBT Thought Challenge

Purpose: Helps identify and challenge distorted thoughts related to body image.

Exercise:

1. Identify the Thought: Whenever you notice a negative thought about your appearance, write it down.

2. Categorize the Distortion: Identify which type of cognitive distortion is at play (e.g., all-or-nothing thinking, catastrophizing).

3. Challenge the Thought: Write a more realistic and balanced thought to counter the negative one.

4. Reflect: Note any changes in your feelings after challenging your thought.

Practical Approach: Exposure Response Prevention Plan

Purpose: To gradually reduce avoidance and compulsive behaviors by confronting feared situations without resorting to rituals.

Steps to Create Your Plan:

1. List Avoided Situations: Write down situations or activities you avoid due to your body image concerns.

2. Rank Them: Order these situations by the level of anxiety they cause.

3. Plan Gradual Exposure: Start with less anxiety-provoking situations. Plan to face these situations and refrain from any compulsive behavior.

4. Reflect and Record: After each exposure, record what happened and how you felt, focusing on any positives you can draw from the experience.

Professional Advice: Lifestyle Adjustments

Advice:

1. Physical Activity: Engage in regular physical exercise that you enjoy. This not only improves physical health but also boosts mental health by reducing anxiety and depression symptoms.

2. Balanced Diet: Focus on a nutritious diet that supports brain function and overall health. Avoid extreme diets that can worsen anxiety about appearance.

3. Quality Sleep: Establish a regular sleep routine to improve both mood and energy levels, making it easier to manage stress and anxiety.

4. Social Connections: Actively maintain and seek out supportive relationships. Share your experiences and struggles when comfortable.

By engaging with these practical approaches and interactive exercises, individuals with BDD can take active steps towards managing their symptoms and improving their quality of life. The provided templates and trackers will help users systematically approach their recovery, making the process more manageable and integrated into their daily lives. This interactive and hands-on method empowers individuals to take control of their journey toward wellness, supported by professional advice and structured guidance.

Cognitive Behavioral Therapy (CBT) for BDD

Cognitive Behavioral Therapy (CBT) is a highly effective treatment for Body Dysmorphic Disorder (BDD). It focuses on identifying, challenging, and changing unhelpful cognitive distortions and behaviors related to one's body image. This section provides a detailed guide on how to implement CBT, including practical exercises that can be used to manage and alleviate symptoms of BDD.

Understanding CBT for BDD

CBT for BDD involves several core components:

1. Education: Learning about BDD and how it affects thoughts, emotions, and behaviors.

2. Cognitive Restructuring: Identifying and challenging negative thoughts related to body image.

3. Behavioral Experiments: Testing out beliefs in real-world situations to reduce avoidance and ritualistic behaviors.

4. Exposure Response Prevention ERP: Systematically facing feared situations related to body image without engaging in compulsive behaviors.

Practical Exercises in CBT

Exercise 1: Thought Record
Purpose: To track and modify distorted thoughts related to appearance.
How to Use: Use a daily log to record situations, initial thoughts, emotions, alternative thoughts, and outcomes.

Example:

Situation: Going to a social gathering.

Automatic Thought: Everyone will notice and laugh at my nose.

Emotion: Anxiety, shame.

Rational Response: People are more likely to focus on their own conversations and enjoyment rather than my appearance.

Outcome: Note any difference in how you feel after replacing the thought.

Exercise 2: Mirror Exposure

Purpose: To reduce the amount of time spent checking appearance and to decrease the associated anxiety.

How to Use: Schedule short, structured periods of mirror exposure daily, gradually increasing the duration and decreasing the frequency of checking.

Example: Start with two 5-minute sessions per day where you look at your reflection in a non-judgmental, neutral way, focusing on your entire self rather than specific features.

Exercise 3: Behavioral Experiments

Purpose: To test the validity of beliefs about perceived defects and the assumptions of others' judgments.

How to Use: Engage in a planned activity that you would normally avoid due to fear of judgment, and record the actual outcomes versus expected outcomes.

Example: Attend a meeting without using makeup or grooming rituals to hide perceived flaws, then note others' reactions and your feelings.

Exercise 4: Role Play

Purpose: To practice and reinforce positive social interactions, reducing social anxiety linked to appearance concerns.

How to Use: With a therapist or trusted individual, role-play social scenarios that are anxiety-inducing, focusing on maintaining conversations and reducing self-focused attention.

Example: Role-play asking someone a question in a group setting and focus on the flow of conversation rather than personal appearance.

Exercise 5: ERP Planning and Implementation

Purpose: To confront feared situations related to body image systematically, without performing rituals.

How to Use: Gradually expose yourself to feared or avoided situations, starting with less anxiety-provoking tasks and building up to more challenging ones.

Example: If you avoid eye contact for fear of face-related defects being noticed, start by making brief eye contact with family, then friends, and slowly progress to strangers or during meetings.

CBT offers a structured approach to tackling the cognitive and behavioral aspects of BDD. Through consistent practice of these exercises, you can learn to manage your symptoms effectively, reduce your preoccupation with appearance, and improve your overall quality of life.

Exposure Response Prevention (ERP) Techniques and Their Application

Exposure Response Prevention (ERP) is a highly effective component of Cognitive Behavioral Therapy (CBT) specifically used for managing obsessive-compulsive behaviors, including those found in Body Dysmorphic Disorder (BDD). ERP involves exposing oneself to the anxiety-provoking stimuli (exposure) and refraining from the compulsive behavior that usually follows (response prevention). This section outlines practical ERP exercises designed to help individuals with BDD confront their fears directly and learn to manage the anxiety without resorting to avoidance or other safety behaviors.

Key Principles of ERP

1. Gradual Exposure: Starting with less anxiety-inducing situations and gradually progressing to more challenging ones.
2. Consistent Practice: Regular practice is crucial to effectively reducing anxiety over time.

3. Response Prevention: Actively resisting the urge to engage in compulsive behaviors during and after exposure.

Practical ERP Exercises for BDD

Exercise 1: Structured Mirror Exposure
Purpose: To reduce the time spent checking and the anxiety associated with mirror gazing.

How to Use:
Step 1: List scenarios where you check your appearance (e.g., before leaving the house, using bathroom mirrors).
Step 2: Choose one scenario and set a timer for a brief, defined period (start with 1-2 minutes) to look at your reflection. Gradually reduce this time over sessions.
Step 3: Observe and record your feelings and thoughts without engaging in any form of checking other than during these scheduled times.

Exercise 2: Photo Exposure

Purpose: To confront anxiety about how one appears in photos, a common trigger for individuals with BDD.

How to Use:

Step 1: Have someone take several photos of you in various settings.

Step 2: Schedule a time to view these photos for a brief period, increasing the duration over time.

Step 3: Note the anxiety levels before, during, and after viewing and avoid any reassurance-seeking or ruminating behaviors.

Exercise 3: Social Exposure

Purpose: To reduce avoidance of social situations due to fears about appearance.

How to Use:

Step 1: Identify social activities you avoid and rank them by anxiety level.

Step 2: Start by attending low-anxiety social events, gradually working up to more anxiety-inducing gatherings.

Step 3: Stay in the situation until your anxiety decreases, and resist any urges to seek reassurance about your appearance.

Exercise 4: Shopping for Clothes

Purpose: To tackle avoidance of fitting rooms and buying clothes, which can be distressing for someone with BDD.

How to Use:
Step 1: Plan a trip to a clothing store but decide in advance not to use the fitting room.
Step 2: On subsequent visits, use the fitting room but limit the time spent inside.
Step 3: Reflect on the experience, focusing on managing discomfort rather than on how the clothes make you look.

Exercise 5: Avoiding Camouflage

Purpose: To reduce reliance on makeup, hats, or other items used to conceal perceived flaws.

How to Use:
Step 1: Identify one item you frequently use for camouflage (e.g., hats, heavy makeup).

Step 2: Gradually reduce the use of this item, starting with safe environments like at home with family.

Step 3: Extend these periods into more public spaces as confidence builds.

ERP is a challenging yet profoundly effective technique for overcoming the compulsive behaviors associated with BDD. By gradually facing feared situations and resisting the urge to engage in compulsive behaviors, individuals can significantly reduce their symptoms of BDD. These practical exercises are designed to be implemented progressively, allowing individuals to build confidence and regain control over their behaviors and thoughts. Through diligent practice, ERP can lead to meaningful improvements in coping with BDD.

Chapter 5

Skill-Building Exercises for Reshaping Thoughts and Behaviors in Body BDD

Developing skills to reshape thoughts and behaviors is crucial for managing Body Dysmorphic Disorder (BDD). This section of the workbook focuses on practical exercises and worksheets designed to help individuals identify, monitor, and change their thought patterns and behavioral triggers. These tools are meant to empower individuals to take active steps towards recovery by understanding and modifying the cognitive and behavioral aspects of BDD.

Cognitive Restructuring and Behavioral Modification

Cognitive restructuring is a fundamental element in Cognitive Behavioral Therapy (CBT) that involves identifying and challenging negative or distorted thoughts that contribute to BDD. Behavioral modification focuses on changing maladaptive behaviors related to these thoughts. Below are exercises and worksheets that facilitate both processes.

Exercise: Daily Behavioral Experiment
Purpose: To test and modify the beliefs related to BDD by engaging in behavioral experiments.

How to Use:
Step 1: Identify a belief related to a perceived flaw or the necessity of a ritual.

Step 2: Design an experiment where you modify your usual response to this belief (e.g., going out without covering up the perceived flaw).

Step 3: Execute the experiment and observe the outcomes—what was the reaction of others, how did you feel during and after?

Step 4: Record the results in a journal and discuss them during therapy sessions or self-reflection periods.

Exercise: Mindfulness and Acceptance Practice

Purpose: To cultivate a non-judgmental awareness of present experiences, reducing the impact of negative thoughts.

How to Use:

Daily Practice: Dedicate a few minutes each day to mindfulness meditation, focusing on breath and bodily sensations, and observing thoughts and feelings without judgment.

Reflection: Keep a journal to note any changes in your relationship with thoughts and feelings about your body image.

These skill-building exercises are designed to provide a structured approach to identifying, understanding, and modifying the cognitive and behavioral patterns associated with BDD. By regularly using these tools, individuals can develop greater self-awareness and control over their thoughts and behaviors, leading to improved coping skills and a reduction in the symptoms of BDD. These practices are essential for anyone working towards recovery from BDD, offering a proactive way to engage with and manage the disorder.

Behavioral Exercises to Reduce Ritualistic Behaviors in BDD

Ritualistic behaviors in Body Dysmorphic Disorder (BDD) can include excessive grooming, mirror checking, or repeatedly seeking reassurance about one's appearance. These behaviors are often performed to reduce anxiety caused by perceived flaws, but they typically only provide temporary relief and can reinforce the disorder. Here, we will explore behavioral exercises designed to help individuals reduce these ritualistic behaviors, fostering healthier coping mechanisms and reducing the overall impact of BDD on daily life.

Behavioral Exercise 1: Scheduled Mirror Checking

Purpose: To gradually decrease the frequency and duration of mirror checking.

How to Use:

Step 1: Log your current mirror-checking habits to establish a baseline.

Step 2: Set specific times of the day for mirror checking, reducing the number gradually. For example, if you currently check your reflection 10 times a day, reduce it to scheduled checks 3 times a day.

Step 3: Use a timer to limit each mirror session to a maximum of one minute.

Step 4: Record feelings and thoughts during non-checking times to monitor anxiety levels and thought patterns.

Benefit: This exercise helps regain control over compulsive checking and reduces the anxiety associated with not being able to check mirrors frequently.

Behavioral Exercise 2: Delay and Distract Technique

Purpose: To delay the urge to engage in a ritualistic behavior and distract oneself with a healthier activity.

How to Use:

Step 1: When the urge to perform a ritualistic behavior arises, set a delay timer (start with 5 minutes and gradually increase).

Step 2: During the delay, engage in a distracting activity that requires concentration or physical engagement, such as reading, walking, or a hobby.

Step 3: After the timer ends, assess the urge level again; often, the urge decreases after engaging in another activity.

Step 4: Gradually increase the delay time as your tolerance improves.

Benefit: This exercise builds tolerance to the discomfort of not performing the ritual and decreases dependency on ritualistic behaviors.

Behavioral Exercise 3: Exposure Journaling

Purpose: To confront the anxiety associated with perceived flaws without resorting to rituals.

How to Use:

Step 1: Write down a detailed description of the perceived flaw without engaging in any rituals to fix or check it.

Step 2: Reflect on the emotions and thoughts that arise when focusing on the flaw in writing.

Step 3: Reframe each negative thought into a more positive or realistic one.

Step 4: Regularly review and update the journal as perceptions and emotions evolve.

Benefit: Journaling about the exposure helps process emotions cognitively and reduces the perceived need for rituals by confronting fears directly.

Behavioral Exercise 4: Habit Reversal Training

Purpose: To replace a ritualistic behavior with a competing response that is incompatible with the ritual.

How to Use:

Step 1: Identify the ritualistic behavior and the conditions under which it occurs.

Step 2: Choose a competing behavior that can be performed instead (e.g., clenching fists instead of picking skin).

Step 3: Practice the competing response every time the urge for the ritualistic behavior is triggered.

Step 4: Keep a log of successes and challenges in implementing the competing response.

Benefit: This technique directly counters the ritualistic behavior with a physical action that makes performing the ritual impossible, thereby breaking the habit loop

.

These behavioral exercises are designed to help individuals with BDD manage and reduce ritualistic behaviors that contribute to the cycle of anxiety and compulsion associated with the disorder. By systematically implementing these exercises, individuals can develop more effective coping strategies, reduce their reliance on rituals, and improve their overall quality of life.

Mindfulness-Based Strategies for Body Acceptance in BDD

Mindfulness involves focusing on the present moment while calmly acknowledging and accepting one's feelings, thoughts, and bodily sensations. For individuals with Body Dysmorphic Disorder (BDD), incorporating mindfulness-based strategies can be a powerful tool for fostering body acceptance and reducing the distress associated with negative body image. Here, we explore practical mindfulness exercises designed to enhance body acceptance and interrupt the cycle of obsessive thoughts about appearance.

Mindfulness Exercise 1: Body Scan Meditation

Purpose: To develop a greater awareness of the body without judgment and to cultivate acceptance of all body parts.

How to Use:

Step 1: Find a quiet, comfortable place to sit or lie down.

Step 2: Close your eyes and take a few deep breaths to ground yourself.

Step 3: Slowly bring your attention to your feet and gradually move up to the top of your head, noticing any sensations, tension, or discomfort without trying to change anything.

Step 4: Whenever you notice judgmental thoughts about a body part, gently acknowledge them and return your focus to the sensations in that part of the body.

Step 5: Conclude the session by reflecting on the experience, acknowledging the body as a whole without focusing on any perceived flaws.

Benefit: This practice helps to connect with the body in a non-judgmental way, reducing the habitual pattern of critiquing one's appearance.

Mindfulness Exercise 2: Mindful Mirror Gazing

Purpose: To change the interaction with mirrors from a source of stress to a moment of mindfulness.

How to Use:

Step 1: Stand in front of a mirror with the intention of observing yourself mindfully.

Step 2: Look at your reflection with curiosity, noticing features with neutrality rather than evaluation.

Step 3: If critical thoughts arise, acknowledge them and then bring your attention back to observing yourself as you might look at a friend, with kindness and acceptance.

Step 4: Practice this for a few minutes each day, gradually increasing the duration as it becomes more comfortable.

Benefit: This exercise can help reduce the anxiety and negative thoughts typically triggered by mirror checking, fostering a kinder, more accepting relationship with one's image.

Mindfulness Exercise 3: Gratitude Body Journaling

Purpose: To shift focus from what you dislike about your body to what it allows you to do, fostering gratitude and appreciation.

How to Use:

Step 1: Each day, write down three things that you appreciate about your body (e.g., "My legs allow me to walk my dog every day").

Step 2: Focus on the function and health of your body rather than appearance.

Step 3: Reflect on these positive aspects regularly and whenever you find yourself slipping into negative thought patterns about your body.

Benefit: Regular gratitude journaling can shift perspective from critical assessments of appearance to a more holistic appreciation of the body's capabilities and strengths.

Mindfulness Exercise 4: Compassionate Self-Talk

Purpose: To develop a more compassionate internal dialogue about one's body, replacing criticism with kindness.

How to Use:

Step 1: Notice when you have a critical thought about your body.

Step 2: Pause and consider what you would say to a friend who expressed this thought about themselves.

Step 3: Redirect this compassionate response to yourself, speaking internally with kindness and understanding.

Step 4: Regularly practice this, especially in challenging situations, to gradually transform how you relate to yourself.

Benefit: This practice helps to break the habit of harsh self-criticism, replacing it with a supportive and nurturing attitude toward one's body.

Integrating mindfulness into daily routines offers a valuable approach for individuals with BDD to develop healthier relationships with their bodies. These exercises not only aid in reducing obsessive and negative thoughts about appearance but also enhance overall mental well-being by promoting acceptance, reducing anxiety, and cultivating a compassionate view of oneself.

Chapter 6

Overcoming Social Stigma for BDD

Dealing with Body Dysmorphic Disorder (BDD) not only involves managing personal symptoms but also confronting the public misconceptions and stigma associated with the disorder. Building strong support networks is crucial for individuals with BDD, as these networks can provide emotional support, reduce feelings of isolation, and help combat stigma. This section outlines strategies to effectively handle public misconceptions and to foster supportive, understanding communities.

Strategies for Dealing with Public Misconceptions and Stigma

1. Educating Others

Purpose: To counteract stigma by providing accurate information about BDD.

How to Use:

- Share resources and information about BDD with friends, family, and colleagues.

- Participate in or organize community talks or workshops to educate others about the realities of BDD.
- Use social media platforms to spread awareness and correct common myths about mental health and BDD.

2. Advocacy

Purpose: To promote understanding and support for BDD at a broader societal level.

How to Use:

- Join or form advocacy groups that focus on mental health and BDD.
- Engage with policymakers to encourage the development of supportive mental health policies.
- Collaborate with mental health professionals to create informative content that can be distributed in schools, workplaces, and health centers.

3. Being Open About One's Experiences

Purpose: To humanize the disorder and reduce stigma through personal stories.

How to Use:

- Share your own experiences with BDD in supportive environments that can foster understanding and empathy.
- Write blogs or articles that detail your journey with BDD, highlighting the challenges and successes.
- Participate in peer support groups where experiences are shared openly and safely.

4. Engaging in Peer Support

Purpose: To build a network of individuals who understand and can relate to the experience of living with BDD.

How to Use:

- Join online forums and support groups specifically for BDD or related mental health issues.
- Attend local support group meetings or start one if none exists in your area.
- Volunteer your time to support organizations that help individuals with BDD.

Combating the stigma associated with BDD is essential for managing the disorder effectively. By educating others, advocating for greater understanding, sharing personal experiences, and cultivating supportive relationships, individuals with BDD can create a more accepting environment. This supportive backdrop not only enhances personal well-being but also empowers individuals to advocate for broader societal change in the perception and treatment of BDD.

Chapter 7

Relapse Prevention and Sustaining Recovery in BDD

Achieving recovery from Body Dysmorphic Disorder (BDD) is a significant milestone, yet sustaining this recovery is equally crucial. This chapter focuses on relapse prevention—a key component for ensuring long-term success in managing BDD. Understanding how to identify potential relapse triggers and effectively manage them can help maintain the progress you've made.

Understanding Relapse

Relapse in BDD involves a return of obsessive thoughts and compulsive behaviors about perceived physical flaws after a period of improvement. It can be discouraging and is often triggered by specific stressors that reignite old thought patterns. However, with the right strategies, relapse can be prevented or managed effectively.

Identifying Potential Relapse Triggers

High-Stress Situations: Stress is a common trigger for many mental health issues, including BDD. Significant life changes, work stress, or relationship problems can all serve as catalysts for a relapse.

Media Exposure: Exposure to media that perpetuates idealized body images can trigger dissatisfaction with one's appearance and reignite BDD symptoms.

Significant Life Events: Milestones such as anniversaries or major life events can evoke strong emotions and stress that may contribute to relapse.

Social Isolation: Reduced interaction with supportive friends and family can increase feelings of loneliness and anxiety, leading to increased risk of relapse.

Changes in Treatment: Altering or discontinuing treatment strategies without professional guidance can lead to a resurgence of BDD symptoms.

Strategies for Managing Relapse Triggers

Stress Management: Developing robust stress management techniques such as mindfulness, regular physical activity, or engaging in hobbies can help mitigate the impact of stress on your mental health.

Critical Media Consumption: Becoming a critical consumer of media and setting boundaries around media use can reduce the impact of harmful beauty standards and unrealistic body images.

Maintaining Social Connections: Keeping a strong support network is vital. Regular contact with friends, family, or support groups can provide emotional support and decrease feelings of isolation.

Consistent Treatment: Continued adherence to treatment plans, including therapy and medications, is crucial for sustained recovery.

Regular check-ins with healthcare providers can help adjust treatments as needed and provide support during challenging times.

Education and Advocacy: Educating oneself and others about BDD can reduce stigma and promote understanding. Advocacy for broader awareness can also reinforce your own recovery journey and help others.

Maintaining Recovery

Sustaining recovery from BDD requires ongoing effort and vigilance. Regularly revisiting and revising coping strategies, maintaining healthy routines, and staying connected with your support system are all essential practices. Recognizing the signs of potential relapse early and responding proactively ensures that recovery remains on track.

Long-Term Coping Strategies and Life Skills for Sustaining Recovery in BDD

Maintaining long-term recovery in Body Dysmorphic Disorder (BDD) involves developing and implementing a set of sustainable coping strategies and life skills. These approaches are designed to help individuals manage symptoms over the long haul, minimize the risk of relapse, and enhance overall well-being. This section of the workbook outlines essential strategies and skills that contribute to sustained recovery and ongoing management of BDD.

Developing Effective Coping Strategies

1. Routine Management:

Purpose: Establishing and maintaining a structured daily routine can significantly enhance feelings of stability and predictability, which are crucial for mental health.

Implementation: Incorporate consistent times for waking up, meals, exercise, social activities, and sleep. Regular check-ins with mental health professionals should also be part of this routine.

2. Cognitive Reframing:

Purpose: Learning to identify and change negative thought patterns can prevent them from escalating into obsessive thoughts.

Implementation: Use tools like thought diaries or cognitive restructuring worksheets to practice reframing negative thoughts about appearance into more positive or realistic ones on a regular basis.

Essential Life Skills for Sustaining Recovery

1. Emotional Regulation Skills:

Purpose: Enhancing the ability to manage and respond to intense emotions in a healthy way is critical for preventing overreaction to body image stressors.

Implementation: Techniques such as deep breathing exercises, progressive muscle relaxation, and emotional journaling can be useful. Training in these skills should be sought through workshops, therapy sessions, or online courses.

2. Social Skills Training:

Purpose: Improving interpersonal skills helps in building and maintaining healthy relationships, which support recovery and reduce isolation.

Implementation: Participate in social skills workshops or group therapy sessions. Practice assertive communication and active listening skills with friends or in a supportive group setting.

3. Problem-Solving Skills:

Purpose: Being able to effectively solve problems that arise in daily life can reduce anxiety and stress that might trigger BDD symptoms.

Implementation: Learn and practice problem-solving techniques, which can be applied to both everyday issues and more significant life challenges. Steps include identifying the problem, brainstorming potential solutions, evaluating these solutions, and then implementing the best option.

Sustaining Recovery Through Lifestyle Adjustments

1. Physical Health Maintenance:

Purpose: Physical health significantly impacts mental health. Maintaining a healthy body through diet and exercise can improve mood and energy levels, which support overall well-being.

Implementation: Adopt a balanced diet, regular exercise regime, and sufficient sleep schedule. Consult with health professionals to create a plan that suits your individual health needs.

2. Continuous Learning and Personal Development:

Purpose: Engaging in lifelong learning and personal development activities can provide a sense of purpose and fulfillment, diverting focus from body image concerns.

Implementation: Take up new hobbies, enroll in educational courses, or engage in creative activities such as writing, painting, or playing music.

Implementing these long-term coping strategies and life skills is vital for anyone recovering from BDD. These approaches not only aid in managing symptoms but also contribute to building a resilient, fulfilling life. By continually practicing and refining these skills, individuals can maintain their recovery and enjoy a robust sense of well-being.

Chapter 8

Final Words of Support and Empowerment

As we reach the conclusion of this workbook, it's important to reflect on the journey you've embarked upon. Recovering from Body Dysmorphic Disorder (BDD) is a path that requires courage, commitment, and continuous effort. You've learned a multitude of strategies, engaged in deep self-reflection, and committed to practices that foster both healing and growth. This final chapter is dedicated to offering you words of support and empowerment to carry forward as you continue on your path to wellness.

First and foremost, recognize the incredible strength it has taken to confront and work through the challenges of BDD. You have shown remarkable resilience and determination. Remember, recovery is not a linear process; there will be ups and downs, triumphs and setbacks. Each step, no matter how small, is a part of your progress towards a healthier, more fulfilled life.

You are not defined by your disorder. You are a unique individual with strengths and capabilities, and you have the power to define who you are and who you want to become. Continue to use the tools and techniques you've learned here to not just manage symptoms, but to build a life that resonates with joy and purpose.

Isolation can be a significant challenge in BDD. Keep nurturing the relationships that support you and consider expanding your support network. Engaging with community groups, continuing therapy or support meetings, and staying connected with loved ones are all essential for sustained mental health. Remember, asking for help when you need it is not a sign of weakness but of strength.

The end of this workbook is not the end of your learning. Continue to educate yourself about BDD and mental health. The field is always evolving, with new research and insights developing regularly. Staying informed can help you adjust your coping strategies as needed and keep you empowered in managing your health.

Thank you for allowing this workbook to be a part of your journey toward recovery. May you continue to find strength, embrace challenges with courage, and live each day with hope and determination. Remember, your journey is one of profound courage, and every step forward, no matter how small, is a victory.

Made in United States
Orlando, FL
11 December 2024